ANNI ALBERS

ANNI ALBERS

by Gene Baro

with an essay

by Nicholas Fox Weber

The Brooklyn Museum

Published for the exhibition
Anni Albers: Drawings and Prints
The Brooklyn Museum
October 1-November 11, 1977

Front cover:
Do V 1973
From the series "Domberger"
Screenprint, 19 x 19 (25 5/8 x 25 5/8). Ed: 50
Collection: The artist
Catalogue #67

Back cover:
Study for Hooked Rug 1964
Gouache, 23 x 17 13/16 (25 1/2 x 18)
Collection: The artist
Catalogue #11

Designed and published by The Brooklyn Museum
Division of Publications and Marketing Services,
Eastern Parkway, Brooklyn, New York 11238.
Printed in the USA by The Falcon Press, Philadelphia.

ISBN 0-87273-062-X
Library of Congress Catalog Card Number 77-82324

FOREWORD

In the textile work of Anni Albers we found many things to delight and intrigue us. Working with the relationships of shape, texture, line, and form—even the very texture of the threads themselves—her work has kept us entranced and hungry for more. She attacked weaving with an energy and passion that is no doubt typical of her life. The medium was the focus of and one of the veritable driving forces of her art.

In looking at Anni Albers's graphic work in this new phase of her art, we now have an extraordinary opportunity. As is made clear in the pages that follow, the intensity of her contact with the specifics of graphics forbids the possibility of her reproducing the art of her weaving. In the drawings and prints we have a chance to see an artist tackle new processes; we witness the fireworks that result from the mixing of a mature aesthetic with the challenge of new mediums. She brings to her graphic work the same focus and the same uncompromising search for the essentials of the medium that she brought to weaving.

This is a strong, provocative, intelligent art. It is a delight to the eye and to the mind.

Our thanks go to Gene Baro, whose imagination and ability have again brought us an outstanding exhibition; to Nicholas Fox Weber, who helped gather information for the exhibition and catalogue; and to Olga and Joseph Hirshhorn and Tyler Graphics Ltd., lenders to the exhibition. One of the joys (or concerns) of a one-person exhibition of a living artist is the close contact it demands between a museum and one of its primary constituents. In the case of "Anni Albers: Drawings and Prints," the experience has been one of joy. Besides providing the backbone of the exhibition, Anni Albers graciously and willingly contributed to every aspect of the presentation of this exhibition. It is indeed her show.

Michael Botwinick
Director
The Brooklyn Museum

A CONVERSATION

Orange, Connecticut
Summer 1977

Anni Albers has discovered independence and freedom through the disciplines integral to her chosen artistic mediums. The marking systems of drawing, the threads and mechanics of weaving, the processes of printmaking—these have stimulated her imagination and have led her to visual statements that are discreet, elegant, and powerful. Her intensely personal work is in the mainstream of our modern artistic and intellectual life and declares a strictly human order. In the following conversation, the artist touches a number of her interests and comments upon her creative development.

Gene Baro
Consulting Curator of Prints and Drawings
The Brooklyn Museum

Gene Baro You made your first reputation as a weaver. How did you come to weaving as your means of artistic expression?

Anni Albers That takes us to the Bauhaus days. I joined the Bauhaus as a student in 1922. There was a requirement to join a workshop, of which there were a number available. I was tempted by the glass workshop not only for the material itself but for the fellow I saw from a distance handling that workshop: Josef Albers. Unfortunately, it was decided that one person was sufficient in that workshop and that no other students could be admitted for work there. What was left to me was to choose among workshops in woodwork, metal, wallpainting, and weaving. Metal I felt was too sharp a material for me; wood required great strength in handling; wallpainting meant climbing ladders. . . . Weaving? Weaving I thought was too sissy. I was looking for a real job; I went into weaving unenthusiastically, as merely the least objectionable choice. Later, weaving at the Bauhaus developed a more serious and professional character. Gradually threads caught my imagination.

For sixteen years at the Bauhaus I worked with a weaver's concern with threads as an artistic vehicle, and I was interested greatly in the technique and discipline of the craft. I enjoyed the chance to do experimental work with textiles for industry.

The pieces concerned with the art side are in various museums here and abroad; the technical discipline took me to universities for teaching and for lectures; the laboratory work for industry was taken up by firms concerned with the presentation of high quality textiles. So much for my involvement with threads.

GB Was drawing a part of your preparation for weaving projects?

AA In part only. Weaving is concerned with a horizontal-vertical construction scheme. Sometimes I worked from drawings. I needed to break away and started to explore freer linear forms. Sometimes I did free explorations with threads on the loom. My great breakaway came when my by-then husband, Josef Albers, was asked to work at the Tamarind Lithography Workshop in Los Angeles. As a useless wife, I was just hanging around, until June Wayne, head of the workshop, asked me to try a lithograph myself. I found that, in lithography, the image of threads could project a freedom I had never suspected. Through the generosity of Tamarind, an edition of my first lithographs was made in 1964. To my happy surprise, I was given a fellowship a year later to return for a month and work out a new series.

Once having discovered this new freedom, I was never able to let go. Returning to our home in New Haven, I found that there were no suitable lithographic workshops available. I had to transform my recently acquired passion into yet another medium: silkscreen printing. It meant devising methods in screenprinting to give effects easily achieved in lithography. From then on screenprinting and other printing techniques became my sole mediums.

GB We know that you must have done preparatory drawings for your screenprints. Did you draw by way of preparation for lithography?

AA For lithographs, I first made drawings on paper and then transferred them to stones or zinc plates.

GB Once the drawings were transferred to stones or plates, did you make changes?

AA No. The drawing provided the final image.

GB Do you feel that there are aesthetic differences between weaving and printmaking? Do you work for the same sense of form in the different mediums?

AA Although you may expect a long answer to this, my answer is very short. There is no medium that cannot serve art.

GB I'm really concerned here with intrinsic differences between weaving and printmaking and how you respond to these differences.

AA In weaving, one deals with the surface quality of the threads—rough, smooth, glossy, shiny. You have only a single result if you deal with pictorial weavings. This limits opportunity for exhibition. Also, weaving is not generally recognized as an art, but as a craft. I find that, when the work is made with threads, it's considered a craft; when it's on paper, it's considered art. Exceptions are the great tapestries of the Middle Ages and the Renaissance.

   Prints give me a greater freedom of presentation. The multiplication and exactness of the process of printmaking allow for broader exhibition and ownership of work. As a result, recognition comes more easily and happily—the longed-for pat on the shoulder.

GB How do you develop your images for printmaking? Do they come out of observation, for instance?

AA Just as the word *career* isn't in my vocabulary, so the word *imagery* isn't in it. Both words presuppose a set goal. I believe my things grow. I start and let things develop under my hand.

GB That suggests a linear development, one thing leading to another.

AA Not necessarily. This brings me back to my long years as a weaver, when it was impossible to tell in advance what a particular thread would do in association with others. The same is true of my work with graphic means. I cannot foretell what a thing will be. I don't know it until the final note. I don't look to the right and left at what others have done.

GB Still, the choices you make, even initially, spring from an inner concern. What might that be? Is it, for instance, a concern for order?

AA You are right. It is a concern for order in a not too obvious way, an order puzzling to the onlooker, so that he will return again and again. The order is timeless, as good things ought to be.

GB May I get back to the matter of sources? Does art for you come out of observation? Is it a metaphor of nature?

AA Nature is puzzling in its tremendous variety. It is not reassuring in its answers. Art tries in the organization of its forms to give an assurance that is understandable to us. Art comes from the desire for such a stabilizing reassurance. Again and again, straight lines, right angles, geometric forms are the signatures of man. Illustrations of nature throw us back to puzzling nature.

GB You speak of the experience of art as being timeless. What is your thinking about artistic personality? How do you feel your own manifests itself?

AA Every child sees things as new. He is an artistic personality, as are those who preserve this quality throughout life. Any experience shows itself in a brush stroke, in a pencil mark, knowingly and unknowingly. I am told that my earlier weaving experience somehow is still reflected in my unwoven work, my graphic work. The work is unconscious in the sense that you feel driven by a notion of what may seem, at a particular point, right or wrong in the chosen technique. Consciousness is necessary to order, an order that should not be instantly readable. Mystery is what draws us to art.

GB Do you feel that the particular medium sets limits to the artist's imagination—and to achievement? Is fully exploiting the particular medium important, even imperative, to the making of high art?

AA Quite definitely. On the other hand, medium is a force that stimulates an artist's productive energies. Fully exploiting the medium is one challenge, but breaking the rules is another. My work, experimental in a certain sense, does not carry a whole new direction. It does not exploit shock values in the fashion of today.

    Graphic mediums are still mysteries to me, and I need to be introduced to each one by the experts concerned with helping me. So far I have worked in lithography, screenprinting, intaglio, and aquatint. I especially respect Ken Tyler, publisher and printer, who has worked with me recently and whose expertise and intensity of work deserve my deep gratitude.

My prints, in contrast to those of many other printmakers, are not reproductions of work I have done in other mediums. They are not transcriptions of paintings or weavings, but are developed entirely out of the chosen technique.

GB Having worked in the major print mediums, do you now have a favorite?

AA No. I feel I am still in the exploratory stage with all of them.

ANNI ALBERS

Nicholas Fox Weber

Anni Albers wrote in 1947: "The more we avoid standing in the way of the material and in the way of tools and machines, the better chance there is that our work will not be dated, will not bear the stamp of too limited a period of time and be old-fashioned some day. . . . And it will outlast fashions only if it embodies lasting, together with transitory, qualities.

"Not only the materials themselves which we come to know in a craft, are our teachers. The tools, or the more mechanized tools, our machines, are our guides too."

Since the summer of 1964, the machinery of printing has been one of Anni Albers's major guides. After many years of work as a weaver, she was introduced to the new freedom of printmaking. Her husband, Josef Albers, was working on a print series at the Tamarind Lithography Workshop, and June Wayne, the workshop director, suggested that Anni also try her hand at printmaking. With textiles, she always let thread do what it could; with printmaking she was free to take threadlike forms even further and to continue with some themes she had occasionally explored in gouache since 1947.

In "Line Involvements," her Tamarind portfolio of six prints, she allowed these forms to break out of the horizontal and vertical construction required by weaving. She retained the interlacing of the threads by moving them alternately over and under each other, but achieved additional qualities now possible in her newly chosen medium. By printing the lines twice, first positive and then negative, off-register, she produced an effect resembling an incision in stone. She used acid to produce a cloudy background. Like her weavings, the Line Involvements were the result of manipulating the process and the technique and of exploring the limits and possibilities of her tools. Although she retained the thread image, the prints were by no means transpositions from another medium.

As a beginning student, Anni Albers had worked in traditional figurative and Impressionistic styles. She was first attracted to the possibilities of the straight line and abstraction shortly after she entered the Bauhaus weaving workshop at age twenty-three. She liked precision and clarity—exact, finite forms that could be balanced and harmonized. Abstract art, man's invention, allowed a totality and wholeness that could not be grasped in nature, which is knowable only in parts. Abstraction, organized and finite, could defeat the tyranny of time and the variables of our vision of nature.

For some time a significant straight-line form in her graphic art has been the triangle, which she had explored in weaving. She can use it more freely in drawing and printmaking, where diagonal lines need not be composed step by step from the vertical and the horizontal. She uses the triangle as the individual element from which to build entire organisms. By reducing the elements and then carefully organizing the like components, she has worked to create the sort of order that touches her in the music of Bach and Mozart, in Seurat's drawings, and in some of Klee's paintings.

Anni Albers carefully weights and arranges these components in study sketches, the first small ones often done on graph paper. She organizes without ever allowing repeated series or simple symmetry. Her constructions are full of variation, of a subtle sense of balance that never yields a formula and therefore provides visual exercise and diversion.

She employs subtle systems to strengthen each construction. She allows the rigorous rules of a well-ordered world to guide her toward her goal of clear composition. Systems within nature, rather than the reflection of human anxiety that concerns so many of the abstract artists from whom she stands apart, have pre-occupied her thought.

The basis of her work is visual, but she has been affected by other sources. As a student, she was deeply impressed by Goethe's *Metamorphosis of Plants*, with its inquiry into an underlying system of regularity with modification, in which like units, repeated with variations, make up the structure of entire organisms. More recently, she was similarly intrigued by what she learned about the structure of metal alloys, which are stronger than the tin and copper that compose them because, instead of having a regular sequence of parallel crystals that easily slip apart, they have varying crystals that create an atomic grit. Anni Albers does not directly illustrate these laws, but she did absorb them, and so her work almost unconsciously reflects them. Modestly and intentionally neutral, she transmits patterns as if her "self" is not their origin.

The arrangements in her Triadic prints and drawings reflect a combined precision and irregularity. Never perfectly symmetrical or formularized, these patterns have a seemingly effortless balance in their harmonious rhythm and in their carefully derived proportions and weights. As a result, the prints and drawings playfully puzzle and intrigue the viewer. The works cannot be simplistically grasped all in a moment, but demand repeated looking.

In her ink drawings, Anni Albers has achieved startling variations with triangles composed in solid black or red or from small dots. In her first Triadic prints, *A* and *B* from 1968, she used two colors of screenprinting for the triangles and a third for the background; *C* and *D* of the next year are screenprints of single-color solid triangles against solid backgrounds.

In *Camino Real* of 1967-69 and *TR I* and *TR II*, produced at Gemini in 1970, she again combined colors of screenprint, and in *TR III* she screenprinted the total surface in gold and embossed the triangular design. In her two Fox prints of 1972, she utilized the photo-offset technique of commercial printing to avoid the flatness of screenprinting. Always determined to make use of the process and to let its capabilities dictate the work, she developed the prints as she learned more about what was technically possible. In *Fox I* her handmade pencil strokes were photographically reproduced, and one overall pattern was reversed by a simple photo-mechanical process to create a two-part print. *Fox II* was made by juxtaposing the negative of the opaque (red) pattern of *Fox I* over a velox of it and turning the result ninety degrees; possible only through such technique, this print had no study drawing.

In *W/CO, PO I,* and *PO II*, she used a combination of the photo-offset reproduction of her pencil strokes with an opaque color screenprint triangular pattern over it.

Her Domberger series of 1973 is all screenprint. And in her most recent series, "Triangulated Intaglios," produced at Tyler Graphics in 1976, she used etching and aquatint for the first time. For the etching, she worked on a special "soft-hard" ground, maintaining the immediacy of her hand and adding a textural aspect.

In her earlier, mazelike Meander series of 1970, Anni Albers also had used printing technique to achieve results not possible in another medium. Each of these screenprints went through the press four times, first with a background screen that laid down a solid color, then twice with a design screen in two different positions in the same color (the color becomes deeper each time it overprints itself), and finally with the design screenprinted in another position in a brighter, dominant color (of limited choice because it had to be simultaneously strong and translucent and therefore could contain no white). The endless meander is full of motion on the surface and in depth; it appears to have layers of shadows that imply many light sources.

As in all of her prints, Anni Albers's attention to the possibilities of the mediums and her positive collaboration with the printers have yielded innovative results. Minimizing self-revelation, concentrating on technique and the voices of her vision, she has stuck to her task of transmitting timeless design to the best of her ability. The results are visual resting places, affirmative solutions that refresh in their purity and order.

Drawings

The following catalogue comprises virtually all Anni Albers's major drawings, important preparatory studies, and her full output of prints.

Throughout, dimensions are in inches; height precedes width. The first set of dimensions given represents the image size. Dimensions in parentheses represent the sheet size.

1   **Knot** 1947
     Gouache, 11¼ x 14½ (17 x 20⅛)
     Collection: The artist

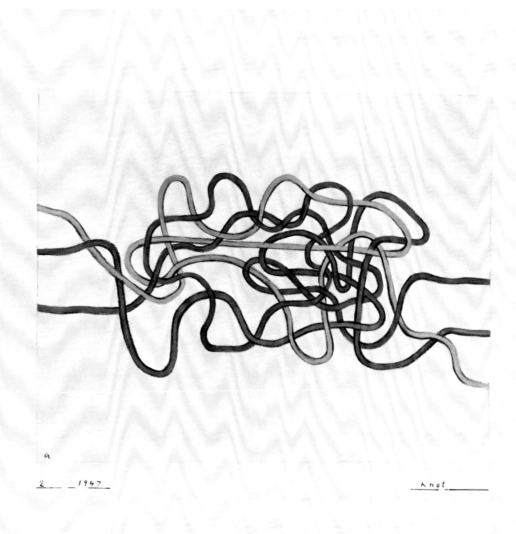

2   **Knot 2** 1947
Gouache, 10⅛ x 13¾ (16⅞ x 19¾)
Private collection

3 **Knot 3** 1947
Gouache, 10⅛ x 14¼ (16½ x 19¾)
Collection: The artist

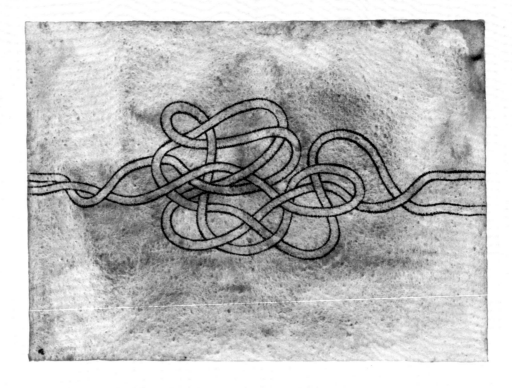

4   **Untitled** 1948
Gouache, 13 ^{13}/$_{16}$ x 10¾ (13 ^{13}/$_{16}$ x 10¾)
Collection: The artist

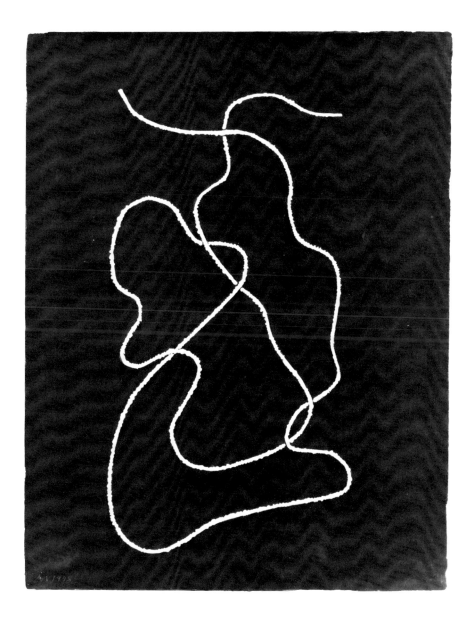

5   **Design** *circa* 1955
     Gouache, 7⅛ x 17¾ (7⅛ x 17¾)
     Collection: The artist

6 **Drawing for Nylon Rug** 1959
Ink on paper, 8½ x 6 ¹/₁₆ (15⅛ x 11⅜)
Collection: The artist

7   **Drawing for a Rug II** 1959
    Ink on paper, 5⅛ x 17³/₁₆ (9⅞ x 24⅜)
    Collection: The artist

Though the drawing is signed for a vertical orientation,
the artist prefers it to be viewed in a horizontal position.

8 **Drawing for a Rug II** 1959
Gouache, 5$\frac{1}{8}$ x 17$\frac{7}{16}$ (9$\frac{1}{8}$ x 22$\frac{1}{16}$)
Collection: The artist

9 **Drawing for a Rug II** 1959
Gouache, 5 1/8 x 17 5/16 (9 1/2 x 22)
Collection: The artist

Anni Albers

10 **Scroll Design** 1960
Ink on paper, 40 x 7 $^1/_{16}$ (42½ x 7¾)
Collection: The artist

11   **Study for Hooked Rug** 1964
      Gouache, 23 x 17 $^{13}/_{16}$ (25½ x 18)
      Collection: The artist

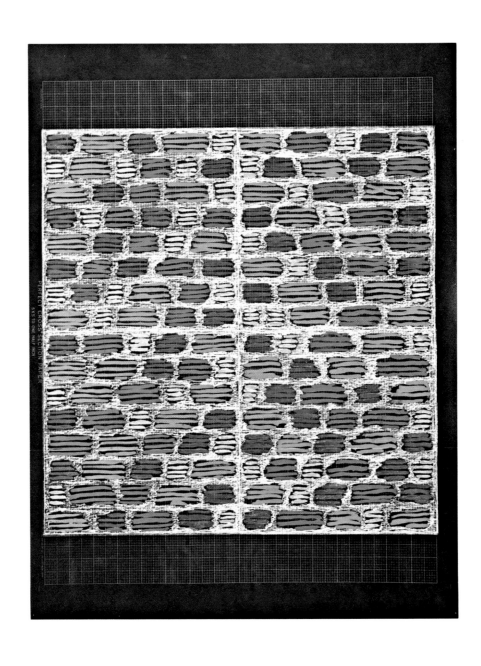

12   **Triadic I Dr. I** (Study for Triadic I) 1968
     Ink and gouache on paper, 13⅛ x 15½
     (14 ¹¹/₁₆ x 17⅜)
     Collection: The artist

The final drawing is in the collection of
Maximilian Schell.

13 **Triadic Dr. II** 1968
Ink on paper, 12⅝ x 12⅝ (17½ x 14⅝)
Collection: The artist

14 **Triadic Dr. III** 1969
Ink on paper, 14 $^{15}/_{16}$ x 14 $^{15}/_{16}$ (20¼ x 17½)
Collection: The artist

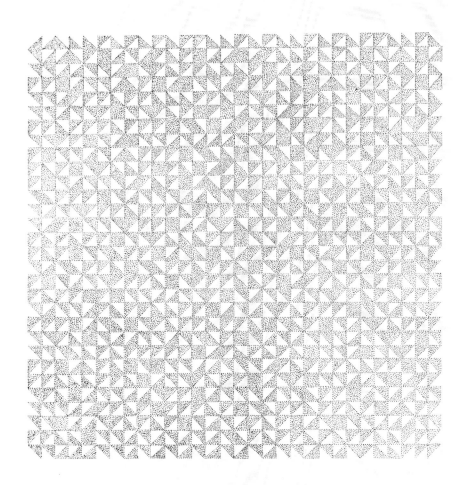

15 **Dr. IV** 1973
   Ink on paper, 4¾ x 14½ (15 x 22¼)
   Collection: Olga Hirshhorn

16 **Dr. V** 1973
   Ink on paper, 4⅝ x 14¼ (15 x 22¼)
   Collection: Olga Hirshhorn

17 **Dr. VI A** 1973
Ink on paper, 15¾ x 14 (29¾ x 22½)
Collection: The artist

18 **Dr. VII** 1973
Ink on paper, 16 x 11 $^{1}/_{16}$ (26 x 20)
Collection: Joseph Hirshhorn

19 **Dr. VIII B** 1973
Ink on paper, 12^9/$_{16}$ x 10^{15}/$_{16}$ (22^3/$_8$ x 15^1/$_{16}$)
Collection: The artist

20 **Dr. IX** 1973
   Ink on paper, 15⅛ x 15½ (30¼ x 22½)
   Collection: Joseph Hirshhorn

21 **Dr. X** 1973
Ink on paper, 13⅛ x 11½ (30⅛ x 22⅜)
Collection: Joseph Hirshhorn

22 **Dr. XI** 1973
Ink on paper, 14½ x 13¹⁵/₁₆ (30¹/₁₆ x 22¼)
Collection: The artist

23 **Dr. XIII** 1974
    Ink on paper, 8 x 14 $^5/_{16}$ (15 $^1/_8$ x 22 $^1/_2$)
    Collection: The artist

24 **Dr. XIV** 1974
    Ink on paper, 4½ x 14 ¹¹/₁₆ (15⅛ x 22⅜)
    Collection: The artist

25　**Dr. XV** 1974
　　Ink on paper, 13¾ x 13⅛ (25¼ x 19⅝)
　　Collection: The artist

26 **Dr. XV B** 1974
Ink on paper, 4 $^{13}/_{16}$ x 14$^7/_8$ (15$^1/_8$ x 22$^7/_{16}$)
Collection: The artist

27　**Dr. XVI** 1974
　　Ink on paper, 17⁹/₁₆ x 14¹/₈ (25³/₈ x 19⁵/₈)
　　Collection: The artist

28 **Dr. XVI B** 1974
Ink on paper, $14\,^{11}/_{16}$ x $11\,^{7}/_{8}$ ($22\,^{1}/_{4}$ x $14\,^{7}/_{8}$)
Collection: The artist

29 **Dr. XVII** 1974
    Ink on paper, 14 $^{11}/_{16}$ x 12 (22¼ x 14 $^{15}/_{16}$)
    Collection: The artist

30　**Dr. XVIII** 1974
Ink on paper, 12 ⁹⁄₁₆ x 12 (25³⁄₈ x 19½)
Collection: The artist

31 **Dr. XX** 1975
Ink on paper, 12⅝ x 11½ (25½ x 19½)
Collection: The artist

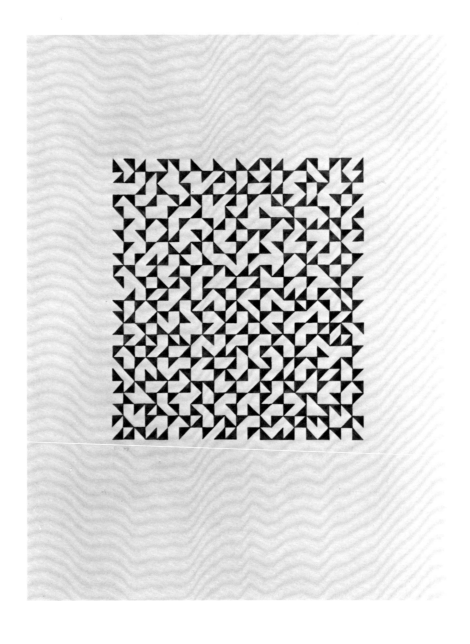

32 **Dr. XXI** 1976
Ink on paper, 8 5/16 x 14¾ (12⅝ x 19½)
Private collection

Prints

33   **Enmeshed I** 1963
Lithograph, 20⅛ x 27³/₁₆ (20⅛ x 27³/₁₆). Ed: 20
Collection: The artist

Published by Tamarind Lithography Workshop.

34 **Enmeshed II** 1963
Lithograph, 17⅛ x 27⅛ (17⅛ x 27⅛). Ed: 20
Collection: The artist

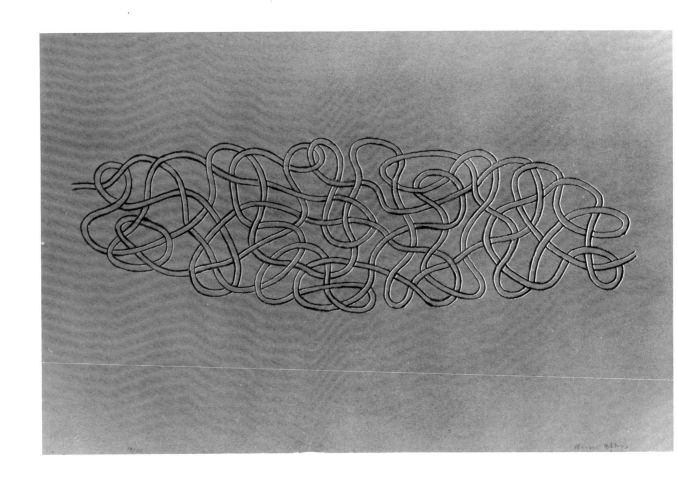

35   **Untitled I** 1963
   Screenprint, 24⅛ x 18¾ (26⅛ x 20). Ed: 75
   Collection: The artist

Published by Tamarind Lithography Workshop.

36 **Untitled II** 1963
Screenprint, 23⅞ x 18½ (26⅛ x 20). Ed: 35
Collection: The artist

37   **Title Page** 1964
From the portfolio "Line Involvements"
Lithograph, 14¾ x 19⅞ (14¾ x 19⅞). Ed: 20
Collection: The Brooklyn Museum
Dick S. Ramsay Fund, 68.226.1

Published by Tamarind Lithography Workshop.

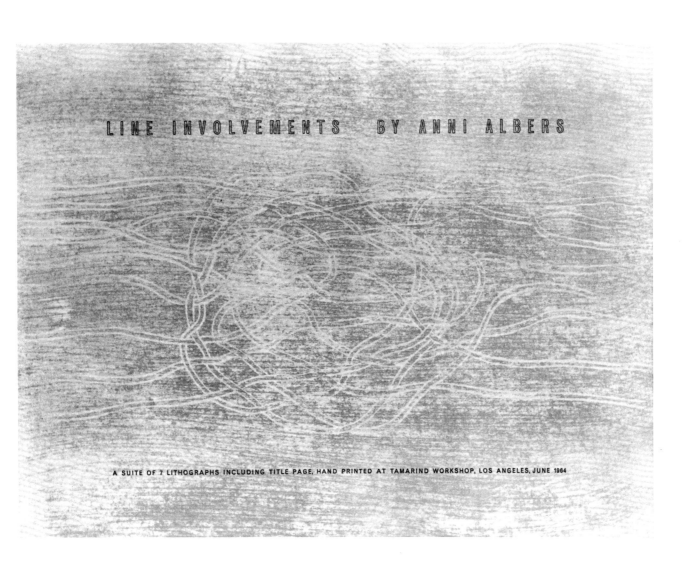

LINE INVOLVEMENTS   BY ANNI ALBERS

A SUITE OF 7 LITHOGRAPHS INCLUDING TITLE PAGE, HAND PRINTED AT TAMARIND WORKSHOP, LOS ANGELES, JUNE 1964

38 **I** 1964
From the portfolio ''Line Involvements''
Lithograph, 19¾ x 14½ (19¾ x 14½). Ed: 20
Collection: The Brooklyn Museum
Dick S. Ramsay Fund, 68.226.2

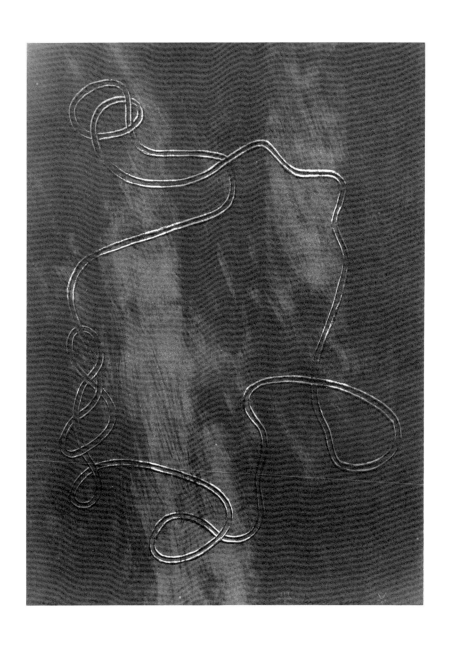

39 **II** 1964
From the portfolio ''Line Involvements''
Lithograph, 14½ x 19¾ (14½ x 19¾). Ed: 20
Collection: The Brooklyn Museum
Dick S. Ramsay Fund, 68.226.3

40　**III** 1964
From the portfolio "Line Involvements"
Lithograph, 19¾ x 14¾ (19¾ x 14¾). Ed: 20
Collection: The Brooklyn Museum
Dick S. Ramsay Fund, 68.226.4

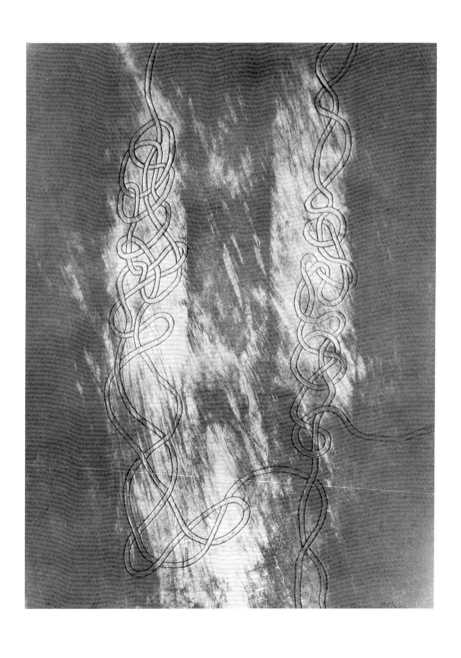

41 **IV** 1964
From the portfolio "Line Involvements"
Lithograph, 14¾ x 19¾ (14¾ x 19¾). Ed: 20
Collection: The Brooklyn Museum
Dick S. Ramsay Fund, 68.226.5

42 **V** 1964
From the portfolio ''Line Involvements''
Lithograph, 19¾ x 14¾ (19¾ x 14¾). Ed: 20
Collection: The Brooklyn Museum
Dick S. Ramsay Fund, 68.226.6

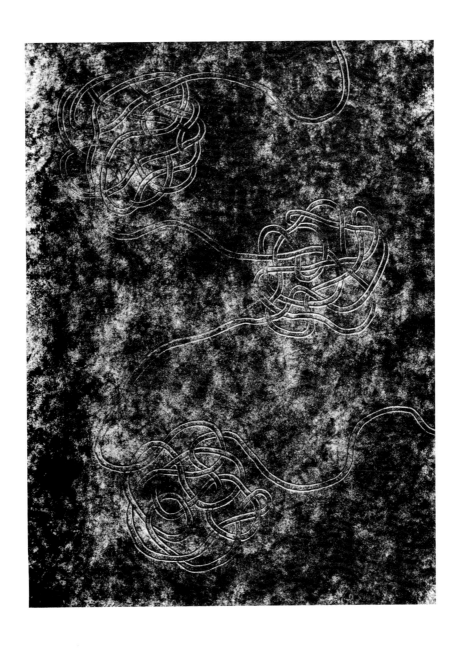

43 **VI** 1964
From the portfolio ''Line Involvements''
Lithograph, 19¾ x 14¾ (19¾ x 14¾). Ed: 20
Collection: The Brooklyn Museum
Dick S. Ramsay Fund, 68.226.7

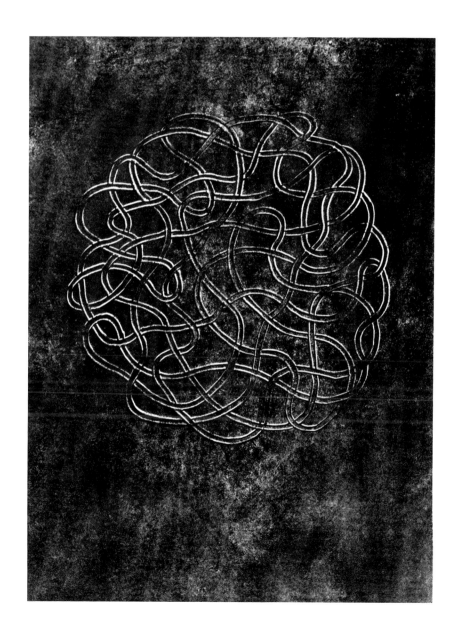

44 **Camino Real** 1967-69
Screenprint, 16 x 15 (23½ x 22). Ed: 90
Collection: The artist

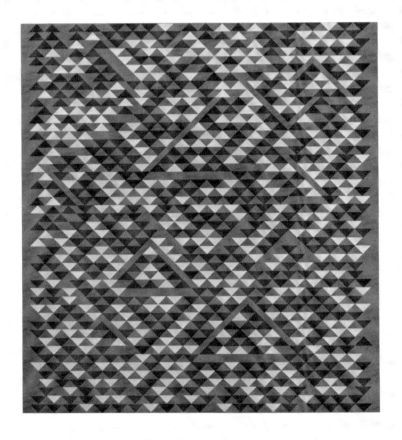

45 **A** 1968
Screenprint, 22 x 18¾ (29⅜ x 25¾). Ed: 50
Collection: The artist

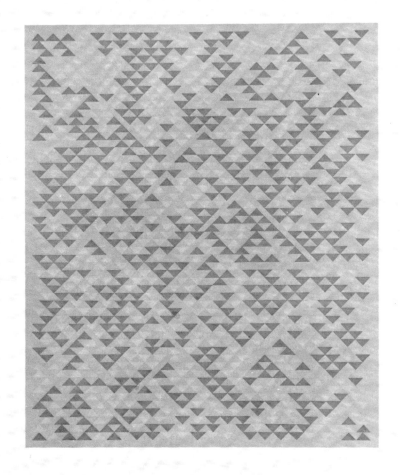

46 **B** 1968
Screenprint, 22 x 18 $^{13}/_{16}$ (29½ x 25 $^{13}/_{16}$). Ed: 50
Collection: The artist

47   **C** 1969
   Screenprint, 17 x 15 (24 x 22). Ed: 65
   Collection: The artist

48 **D** 1969
Screenprint, 17 x 15 (24 x 22). Ed: 60
Collection: The artist

49　**E** 1969
　　Screenprint, 17½ x 16 (24½ x 23). Ed: 60
　　Collection: The artist

50 **F** 1969
   Screenprint, 17½ x 16 (24½ x 23). Ed: 60
   Collection: The artist

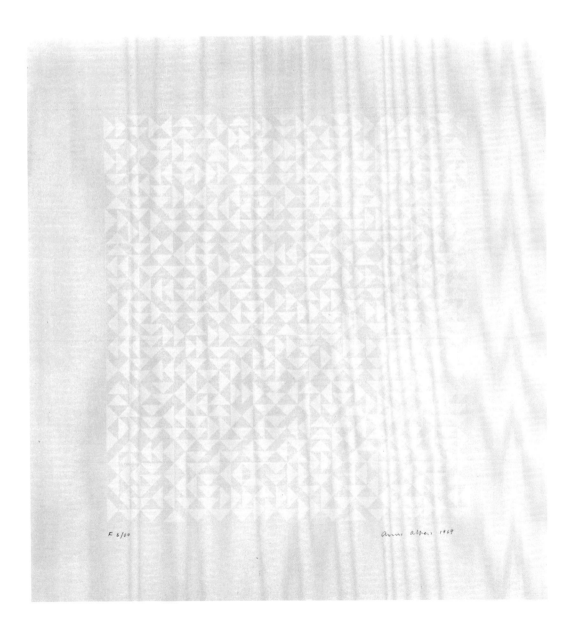

51 **Red Meander** 1969
Screenprint, 20 x 16½ (28 x 24½). Ed: 50
Collection: The artist

52 **Red Meander II** 1970
Screenprint, 20 x 16 (28 x 24). Ed: 75
Collection: The artist

53 **Blue Meander** 1970
Screenprint, 19½ x 16 (28 x 24). Ed: 75
Collection: The artist

54 **Yellow Meander** 1970
Screenprint, 16½ x 16½ (28 x 24). Ed: 75
Collection: The artist

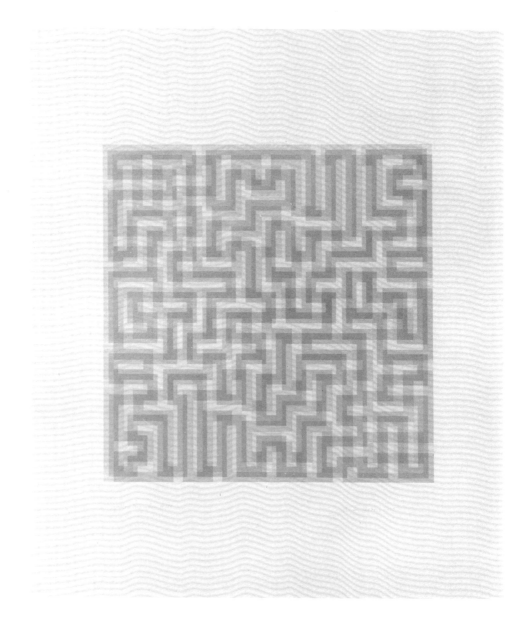

55 **Orange Meander** 1970
Screenprint, 16$\frac{1}{2}$ x 16$\frac{1}{2}$ (28 x 24). Ed: 75
Collection: The artist

56   **TR I** 1970
   Screenprint, 14 x 16 (19¾ x 21⅝). Ed: 50
   Collection: The artist

Published by Gemini GEL.

57 **TR II** 1970
Screenprint, 14 x 16 (19⅞ x 21⅞). Ed: 45
Collection: Tyler Graphics Ltd.

58 **TR III** 1970
   Embossed screenprint, 14 x 16 (16½ x 18½)
   Ed: 60
   Collection: The artist

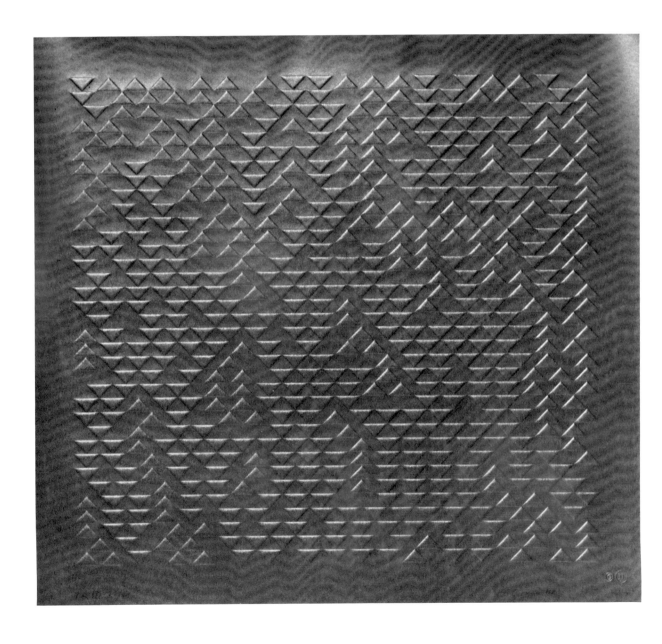

59 **GR I** 1970
Screenprint, 20 x 16 (29 x 24). Ed: 100
Collection: The artist

Published by Joseph Grippi.

60 **ST** 1971
    Screenprint, 18¾ x 16⁹/₁₆ (32¹/₁₆ x 24⅜)
    Ed: unknown
    Collection: The artist

This print is the seventh proof of a special publication of
Galerie Der Spiegel, Cologne.

61 **Fox I** 1972
Photo offset, 14⅞ x 13 ⁷/₁₆ (24 x 20). Ed: 150
Collection: The artist

Published by Fox Press, Inc., and the artist.

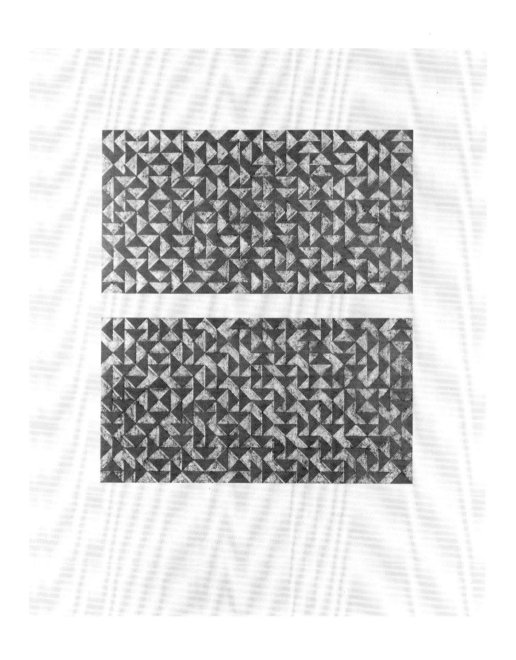

62 **Fox II** 1972
   Photo offset, 13¼ x 14 ^{11}/$_{16}$ (20 x 20). Ed: 150
   Collection: The artist

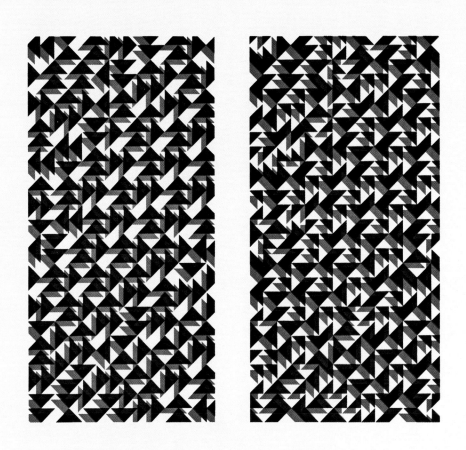

63 **Do I** 1973
From the series "Domberger"
Screenprint, 17 x 17 (25⅝ x 25⅝). Ed: 50
Collection: The artist

Published by Edition Domberger.

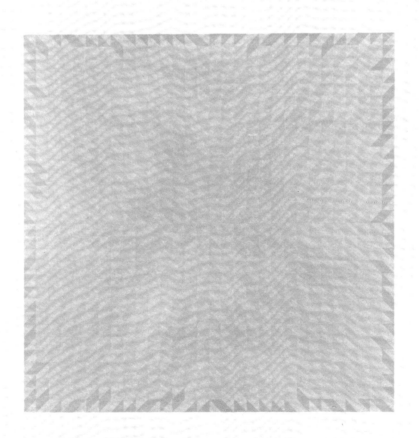

64 **Do II** 1973
From the series "Domberger"
Screenprint, 17 x 17 (25⅝ x 25⅝). Ed: 50
Collection: The artist

65 **Do III** 1973
From the series "Domberger"
Screenprint, 16 x 16 (25⅝ x 25⅝). Ed: 50
Collection: The artist

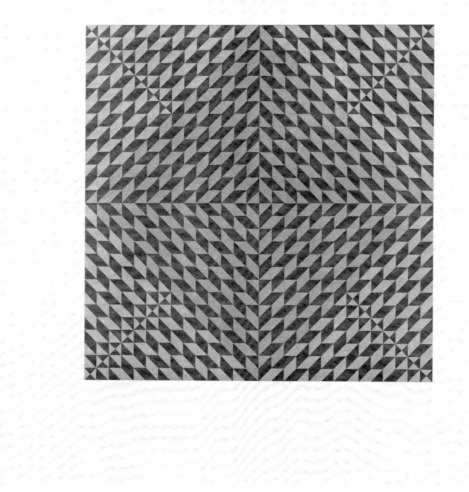

66 **Do IV** 1973
From the series "Domberger"
Screenprint, 19 x 19 (25⅝ x 25⅝). Ed: 50
Collection: The artist

67 **Do V** 1973
From the series "Domberger"
Screenprint, 19 x 19 (25⅝ x 25⅝). Ed: 50
Collection: The artist

Reproduced in color on the front cover.

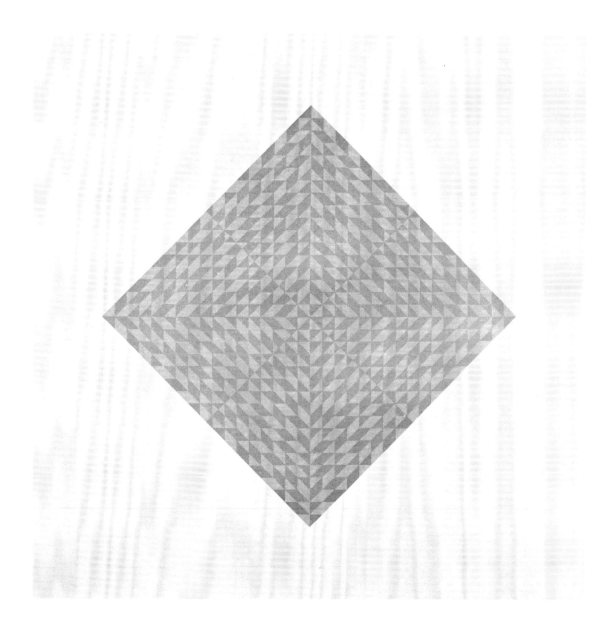

68   **Do VI** 1973
From the series "Domberger"
Screenprint, 16 x 16 (25⅝ x 25⅝). Ed: 50
Collection: The artist

69 **Do X** 1973
Screenprint, 19 x 19 (25⅝ x 25⅝). Ed: 26
Collection: The artist

70 **PO I** 1973
Screenprint and photo offset, 15 x 12½
(28¾ x 22). Ed: 40
Collection: The artist

71 **PO II** 1973
Screenprint and photo offset, 15 x 12½
(28 ¹¹/₁₆ x 22). Ed: 30
Collection: The artist

72 **W/CO** 1974
Screenprint and photo offset, 15 x 12½
(29 ¹³/₁₆ x 22). Ed: 60
Collection: The artist

73 **I** 1976
From the series "Triangulated Intaglios"
Etching and aquatint, 12⅞ x 11¾ (24 x 20⅛)
Ed: 20
Collection: The artist

Published by Tyler Graphics Ltd.

74 **II** 1976
From the series ''Triangulated Intaglios''
Aquatint, 13 x 11⅞ (24 x 20). Ed: 20
Collection: The artist

75 **III** 1976
From the series ''Triangulated Intaglios''
Etching and aquatint, 12¾ x 12 (24 x 20). Ed: 20
Collection: The artist

76 **IV** 1976
From the series "Triangulated Intaglios"
Aquatint, 13 x 11⅞ (24 x 20). Ed: 20
Collection: The artist

77 **V** 1976
From the series "Triangulated Intaglios"
Aquatint, 12⅞ x 11⅞ (24 x 20⅛). Ed: 20
Collection: The artist

78 **VI** 1976
From the series "Triangulated Intaglios"
Etching, 12⅞ x 12 (24 x 20). Ed: 20
Collection: The artist

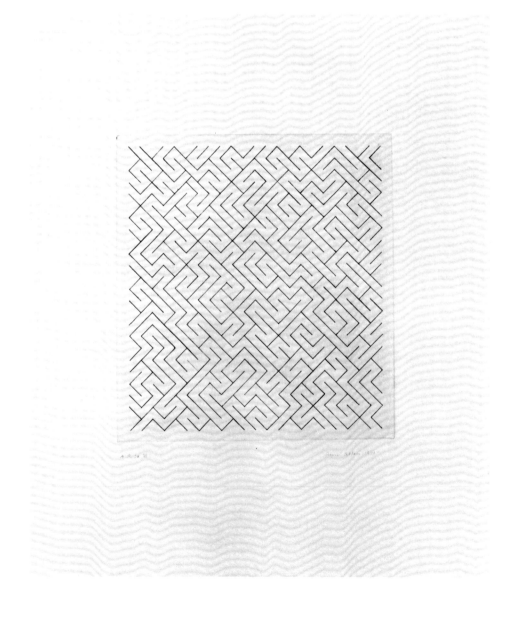

BIOGRAPHICAL OUTLINE

1899	Born in Berlin.
1922-30	Student at Bauhaus in Weimar and Dessau. Bauhaus Diploma.
1933-49	Assistant Professor of Art, Black Mountain College, North Carolina.
1937	Became U.S. citizen.
1950	Moved to Connecticut.
1961	Medal of American Institute of Architects in the Field of Craftsmanship.
1962	Citation, Philadelphia Museum College of Art.
1964	Tamarind Lithography Workshop Fellowship (June).
1965	DABA Citation, The Decorative Arts Book Award.
1972	Degree, Doctor of Fine Arts, *honoris causa*, The Maryland Institute College of Art.
1973	Degree, Doctor of Laws, *honoris causa*, York University, Toronto, Ontario.
1976	Degree, Honorary Degree of Doctor of Fine Arts, Philadelphia College of Art.

One-person exhibitions
The Baltimore Museum of Art, Baltimore, Maryland.
Bauhaus-Archiv, Berlin, Germany.
Carnegie Institute, Pittsburgh, Pennsylvania.
Colorado Springs Fine Arts Center, Colorado Springs, Colorado.
Contemporary Arts Museum, Houston, Texas.
Honolulu Academy of Arts, Honolulu, Hawaii.
Kunstmuseum der Stadt Düsseldorf, Düsseldorf, Germany.
Massachusetts Institute of Technology, Cambridge, Massachusetts.
Museum of Modern Art, New York.
Wadsworth Atheneum, Hartford, Connecticut.
Yale University Art Gallery, New Haven, Connecticut.

Collections—Pictorial weavings
The Art Institute of Chicago, Chicago, Illinois.
The Baltimore Museum of Art, Baltimore, Maryland.
Bauhaus-Archiv, Berlin, Germany.
Busch-Reisinger Museum, Cambridge, Massachusetts.
Cranbrook Academy of Art, Bloomfield Hills, Michigan.
The Currier Gallery of Art, Manchester, New Hampshire.
The Jewish Museum, New York.

The Johnson Wax Collection, Racine, Wisconsin.
Kunstgewerbemuseum der Stadt Zürich, Zürich, Switzerland.
Kunsthalle Nürnberg, Nürnberg, Germany.
The Metropolitan Museum of Art, New York.
Museum of Modern Art, New York.
Neue Sammlung Museum, Munich, Germany.
Städtische Kunstsammlungen, Darmstadt, Germany.
Victoria and Albert Museum, London, England.
Yale University Art Gallery, New Haven, Connecticut.
Et al.

Collections—Graphic work
Art Gallery of Ontario, Toronto, Ontario.
The Brooklyn Museum, Brooklyn, New York.
Busch-Reisinger Museum, Cambridge, Massachusetts.
Fort Worth Art Museum, Fort Worth, Texas.
The Israel Museum, Jerusalem, Israel.
Kunstmuseum der Stadt Düsseldorf, Düsseldorf, Germany.
The Metropolitan Museum of Art, New York.
Museum of Modern Art, New York.
The New York Public Library, New York.
The St. Louis Art Museum, St. Louis, Missouri.
Seattle Art Museum, Seattle, Washington.
University of California, Los Angeles, California.
Wadsworth Atheneum, Hartford, Connecticut.
Westfälisches Landesmuseum für Kunst und Kulturgeschichte, Münster, Germany.
Yale University Art Gallery, New Haven, Connecticut.
Et al.

SELECTED BIBLIOGRAPHY

Books by Anni Albers

On Designing. New Haven, Connecticut: Pellango Press, 1959. Reprint. Middletown, Connecticut: Wesleyan University Press, 1962. Paperback. 1971.

On Weaving. Middletown, Connecticut: Wesleyan University Press, 1965. Reprint. 1972. Paperback. 1974.

Pre-Columbian Mexican Miniatures. New York: Praeger Publishers, 1970.

Exhibition Catalogues

Cambridge, Massachusetts. Massachusetts Institute of Technology. *Anni Albers, Pictorial Weavings,* 1959.

Düsseldorf, Germany. Kunstmuseum Düsseldorf. *Anni Albers,* 1975.

Hartford, Connecticut. Wadsworth Atheneum. *Josef and Anni Albers,* 1953.

Manchester, New Hampshire. The Currier Gallery of Art. *Albers/Callery/Fuller,* 1956.

Books and Periodicals

"Bauhaus." *Offset* (Germany), 1925.

Bauhausler in Amerika. Berlin: Bauhaus-Archiv, 1976.

Constantine, Mildred, and Larsen, Jack Lenor. *Beyond Craft: The Art Fabric.* New York: Van Nostrand Reinhold, 1973.

Delaunay, Sonia. *Tapis et Tissus.* 1926.

Donohoe, Victoria. "Gallery Tour." *Philadelphia Inquirer,* November 12, 1971.

Duberman, Martin. *Black Mountain.* New York: Archer Editions Press, 1973.

"Exhibition at Yale Gallery to Have Pictorial Weavings of a Leading Pioneer Artist." *New Haven Evening Register,* December 8, 1959.

Fisher, Barbara E. Scott. "Anni Albers' Textiles Serve, Not Dominate, Architecture." *Christian Science Monitor,* October 19, 1949.

Gadner, Marilyn. "Designer Creates Orderliness in Nature." *Milwaukee Journal,* November 9, 1956.

"Hanging Panels Offer One Way to Divide Area with Flexibility." *New York Tribune,* September 25, 1949.

Nasgaard, Roald. "Toronto." *Arts Canada,* November, 1973.

Naylor, Gillian. *The Bauhaus.* London: Studio Vista/Dutton, 1968.

"New Dimensions in Lithography." *Arts Magazine,* February, 1965.

Nordness, Lee. *Objects: USA.* New York: Viking Press, 1970.

Rouark, Robert C. "It's Art, Baby." *Philadelphia Evening Bulletin,* February 27, 1946.

Scott, Martha B. "Anni Albers' Art Will Endure Like Her Beloved Clay Idols." *Bridgeport Sunday Post,* February 21, 1971.

Smith, Janet K. *Design: A Laboratory Manual.* Ziff-Davis Publishers, 1945.

Thomas, Howard, and Thomas, Mary. *Design.* 1948.

Weber, Nicholas Fox. "Anni Albers and the Printerly Image." *Art in America,* Summer, 1975.

Welliver, Neil. "A Conversation with Anni Albers." *Craft Horizon,* July/August, 1965.

Wilk, Gerald. *Americans from Germany.* New York: German Information Center, 1977.

Wingler, Hans. *The Bauhaus.* Cambridge, Mass.: M.I.T. Press, 1969.

INDEX TO LENDERS